The Art of Finding Joy Within

New Edition 2024

By

ALEX GIOVANNI BEDOYA

SELF-HELP GUIDES

DISCLAIMER

This book provides suggestions only and how the reader uses it is their choice. The authors /publishers are not liable for inappropriate use of the information by the reader.

CONTENTS

1 UNVEILING INNER JOY

World history overflows with biographies of successful individuals. While success or joy may be relative concepts, everyone can achieve them by staying true to their emotions, passions, and ambitions. History stands as a testament: true success blossoms from love (for a specific pursuit) rather than just relentless, blind labor. In any activity, only those who invest perseverance, responsibility, and most importantly, genuine passion, will find joy.

Indeed, your love, passion, and enterprising spirit can be harnessed to generate wealth beyond your wildest dreams. But more importantly, it significantly reduces effort and stress by allowing you to work on something you truly care about.

However, passion, love, and a sense of duty alone are not enough to guarantee prosperity and fruition. Sometimes, a shift in perspective and a fresh viewpoint are necessary to identify ways to amplify your efforts. Keep your senses open, your mind free from anxieties, and prioritize effectively.

Throughout any endeavor, it is crucial to stay connected to your inner self, the guiding force behind your passions, triumphs, ambitions, desires, and love. Once you have clarity on your goals and ignite the fire of passion within your involvement, you achieve harmony with yourself – the key ingredient in the recipe for joy.

Identify the root causes of stagnation, boredom, or failed endeavors in your pursuits. Confronting your doubts, worries, and anxieties may seem daunting, but it is the only way to combat these negative thoughts. Therefore, a change in perspective will banish boredom and motivate you to view your achievements in a new, confident light.

Instead of questioning your abilities and beliefs, this book empowers you to pursue your joy. We all need to appreciate and understand ourselves, and this book serves as your guide on that journey. It will help you define your goals, equip you with effective strategies for success and true happiness, and along the way, help you generate wealth.

2 **FOLLOW YOUR JOY**

We all carry within us, from our childhood years, ambitions, dreams, and aspirations for how our lives will unfold. Woven throughout these aspirations is a constant yearning for joy, a companion we hope will walk beside us on life's journey. Sometimes, however, the search for happiness feels like a long and arduous trek, demanding relentless effort. Finding joy may seem effortless for some, while others face a challenging climb, their paths marked by life's inevitable stumbles. These stumbles can leave us feeling distressed, unhappy, and lacking. Yet, it is important to remember that financial hardship does not guarantee misery, nor does wealth ensure joy. Joy is not a material possession to be acquired; it is an intangible treasure we cultivate through the power of desire and conscious experience.

Waking up to a day devoid of purpose can be a disheartening experience, twisting our hearts with a sense of emptiness. Conversely, discovering your unique path in life and pursuing it with passion ignites a fire within, illuminating a life overflowing with joy. The journey to happiness is a deeply personal one. No one realizes you are lost until you either seek guidance or find your own way forward.

Pearl Bailey's words resonate with profound truth: 'You never find yourself until you face the truth.'

Indeed, self-deception acts as a barrier to joy. Hiding your vulnerabilities prevents your heart from achieving true honesty. To find joy, take stock of your life. Honestly assess your strengths and weaknesses, and if needed, seek help from others.

The words of Jesus, 'He that finds his life loses it and he that loses his life finds it,' hold profound meaning in your search for joy. A meaningful life, a life pursued with passion and purpose, is a life truly lived. The pursuit of joy transforms the feeling of loss into a vibrant embrace of each moment.

Embarking on the path of self-discovery prepares you not only to find joy for yourself but also to alleviate the suffering you may have once endured in others. Let your heart overflow with the desire for joy. Repeat daily: "I am the happiest person on Earth." This affirmation will reshape your outlook on life. You will begin to see possibility everywhere, fostering a belief that YES, you can find joy!

3 KNOW YOURSELF, FIND JOY

Knowing yourself requires a relentless pursuit of self-discovery. Accurately evaluating yourself is arguably the best way to ensure you are on the right life path. Feeling overworked, time-pressed, or bitter about life might be a sign to ask yourself: "Is this worth my effort?" Take a break from your hectic schedule and confront yourself. You might be surprised how far you have strayed from the picture of success you once envisioned.

Dreams and Motivations

Reconnecting with your childhood dreams and motivations is crucial. Your development and success stem from those formative years. Reflect on where you envisioned yourself 15 years ago. Do not be discouraged if you have strayed from the target. Often, you will find yourself more successful than you ever imagined. However, rekindling the youthful spark that ignited your dreams can be challenging. Regardless of your current position, staying grounded in your core values is paramount. Confidence in your goals and dreams provides a solid foundation for tackling life head-on.

Routines and Regularity

A study by the United States Department of

Agriculture's Center for Nutrition Policy and Promotion emphasizes the importance of maintaining a consistent routine. Living a life of uncertainty and spontaneity might sound romantic, but it is impractical. Planning helps you navigate unforeseen events without feeling disoriented. This means scheduling your days, managing finances and social commitments, and fulfilling your responsibilities.

Even if initial attempts at establishing routines are not perfect, the effort itself demonstrates your readiness to take control. Create small to-do lists and routines, and commit to them for a set period. You will be surprised at how quickly anxieties and last-minute worries fade away.

4 MAXIMIZE YOUR POTENTIAL

An ancient Chinese proverb warns: "The path to self-discovery lies through a thicket of thorns." Indeed, the battle for success is arduous and challenging, but ultimately rewarding. To achieve success in your endeavors, the first place to seek alliance and support is within yourself. Talents alone are insufficient if misused or not strategically deployed. Knowing yourself necessitates a brave appraisal of your talents and abilities. This self-assessment will reveal if your current pursuits align with your strengths, or if a change is necessary.

Confidence is the Key

No talent, skill, or expertise is insignificant if you understand its value and respect the effort invested in acquiring it. While some may be gifted, innate talent alone does not guarantee the expertise, perseverance, or mastery needed to unleash its full potential. Jimmy Hendrix, a prodigy, still had to practice each guitar note countless times before becoming a legendary musician. Deep down, each of us possesses some skill or ability worthy of honing. All you need is conviction and confidence in your abilities to refine them and showcase them to the world. (See: Voodoo Child: The Illustrated Legend of Jimi Hendrix)**

Learning to Love Who You Are

Not everyone is destined to be a genius painter, artist, musician, strategist, theoretician, or poet. There is no need to apologize for your abilities or the extent of your talents.

Talents exist solely to bring happiness and the satisfaction of creation. Recognizing and appreciating your talents is the first step towards using them productively. Focus on your strengths and abilities, for they will equip you to overcome life's difficulties. Embracing your talents will instill a sense of pride and happiness within you, because you are, after all, your own best critic.

Do not be discouraged if your artwork does not hang in exhibitions, your concerts do not sell out, or your novels remain unpublished. Take comfort in knowing you gave it your all and strived for self-improvement. This personal integrity and dedication are paramount, for they shape you into a better, happier, and more confident individual.

5 **WINNING MINDSET**

The two most fundamental requirements for achieving success in life are the ability to ask questions and the power to imagine the answers.

Imagination plays a crucial role in defining your goals, aspirations, ambitions, and even your dreams. It is no coincidence that imagination, creativity, and curiosity are intertwined. Creativity allows you to manifest your imaginings into reality. When you are curious about how things might unfold, you harness your imagination to envision the most viable solutions. The power of imagination is indeed a talent, and one that, when nurtured, will yield rich rewards.

Curiosity compels you to ask questions about the how and why of things. This inquisitiveness is a valuable quality, demonstrating your eagerness to gain a true understanding of life. It may even spark a new passion or a captivating hobby.

Each of us possesses an inner talent, often yearning for an outlet of expression. Perhaps you are a gifted artist whose paintings have not found a platform, or a skilled chess player who has not pursued professional competition. This reluctance to fully express your talents stems from a lack of imagination. Most limitations are not imposed by our talents themselves, but by the ones we create in our minds. Imagination and creativity are the keys to surpassing these self-imposed boundaries.

When we engage our imagination, we dream big. We envision new goals and paths to success. Here, it is critical to maintain focus and avoid distractions. The key lies in finding something that truly aligns with your talents and, once found, embracing it wholeheartedly. This is where you unleash your imagination and creativity, maximizing your joy in the process and boosting your chances of success.

For instance, if you are drawn to colors, why not adorn your walls with vibrant graffiti or a captivating painting? This way, your imagination earns you a personalized, stunning wall, a testament to your creative spirit and a source of joy in your life.

6 **CREATIVE OUTLETS**

Haven't we all witnessed a puzzling situation where a child solves a problem that baffles adults? What, we wonder, is at work here? The answer: intuition.

Most of us do not work in creative fields. In fact, most of us do not. We navigate a mechanized, production-line world. As we become increasingly enmeshed in this rule-bound environment, our creative faculties gradually atrophy. This stifling cause-and-effect mentality ultimately hinders even our work performance.

That is why keeping our creative batteries charged is crucial. Everyone needs to cultivate a hobby, regardless of skill level. Any simple, creative outlet works – painting, playing an instrument, or even cooking for those who enjoy it but rarely have the time. The key is to indulge in something purely for your own enjoyment, not external rewards.

This is not just about enriching your free time. Engaging in creative activities can also improve your work performance. As the example illustrates, these pursuits encourage us to think outside the box. Children often have the answer because their knowledge has not been rigidly categorized into "acceptable" or "taboo." Societal value systems can narrow our perspective, but a creative hobby helps us unlock our minds again. Fortunately, there is no shortage of activities to choose from: hiking for adventurers, sports for the athletic, artistic pursuits for the creative, or even furniture making for those who fancy it!

As we age, we lose the ability to respond to situations as naturally as children do. Creative activities help us re-establish this connection. The freedom of engaging in something non-goal-oriented is immensely beneficial.

There is a sense of fulfillment even if your painting is a bit comical or you lose a football match miserably. If you stop enjoying what you do, your work performance is bound to decline. And let us face it, you are sure to stop enjoying your work if it is the only thing, you do all week. A creative hobby injects a vital change into your lifestyle, pulling you out of a rut. It not only reignites your passion for work but also enhances your ability to perform it effectively.

7 SUCCESS ESSENTIALS

There is perhaps nothing quite as exhilarating and gratifying as success. Remember the time you ranked first in class or were part of a championship-winning team? The feeling of accomplishment likely left everything else fading into the background. Success is truly an immersive experience, a validation of your hard work, passion, and dedicated involvement.

As you might guess, there is no magic formula for becoming super-successful. However, keeping these factors in mind can certainly propel you on the right path to achieving success, if not guaranteeing it.

Confidence and Self-Belief

Confidence is paramount. Only you can be certain of your success. You hold complete control over your talents and abilities, and ultimately, you define your chances of achieving your goals. Believing in yourself is essential. When you rely on your inner strength for support, you cultivate resilience and independence. If self-doubt creeps in, even momentarily, try to recall your most hard-earned moments of personal triumph. If you have embarked on a project, trust that you have the capacity to see it through to completion.

Finding the Right Attitude

Your attitude towards life shapes who you are. It broadcasts your ideas, perceptions, dreams, and aspirations to the world, influencing how others perceive you. Because your attitude is such an integral part of your identity, ensure it aligns with your thoughts and actions. A confident and positive approach is key. If you exude optimism and ease, chances are the world will rally around you. People will only invest their belief in you once you demonstrate your own ability to see the silver lining. This positive outlook will enhance your focus and inner strength, giving you more energy to pursue success.

Planning and Pacing Your Life

Knowing when to push forward and when to take a breather is crucial. Striking the right balance between lethargy and hyperactivity is essential. If you have a three-day deadline for an assignment, do not get swept away by the urge to finish it in one day. Take that extra time for meticulous planning and solid execution. Pacing yourself and your actions will make you a more capable and clear-headed individual, ultimately leading to a fulfilling life.

8 HEALTHY BODY, HAPPY MIND

Happiness Defined

Joy can be defined as a state of sustained satisfaction and elation. Public perception often equates happiness with constant exuberance – always smiling and perpetually content. However, scientists and psychologists view happiness as a psychosomatic state triggered by specific hormone releases tied to a particular mental state. When your body is relaxed and at peace, your mind likely follows suit. Achieving this state of complete unity and synchronicity between body and mind is what constitutes true happiness.

Factors Influencing Happiness

Healthy Lifestyle

A healthy, active lifestyle empowers you with greater control over your body, boosting your overall health and fitness. It keeps your body functioning optimally, providing you with more energy and stamina to tackle life's challenges. Engaging in regular physical activity, like running, swimming, or participating in sports, strengthens your immune system and enhances the function of your sensory organs, heart, lungs, and digestive system. This translates to a healthier and more fulfilling life, free from the constant worry about diseases like diabetes, obesity, and heart problems.

With a healthy body, you have more energy to spend quality time with loved ones, pursue hobbies, and celebrate life's joys. Additionally, a healthy lifestyle involves kicking addictions like smoking and excessive alcohol consumption.

Regulated Sleep

Just like infants and older adults, adults also require their daily dose of sleep. Scientific research suggests that the average working adult needs 7 to 9 hours of sleep per night. This period is crucial for the body to repair itself and lower its metabolic rate. Sound sleep rejuvenates both your body and mind, replenishing your energy and clearing away stress, anxiety, and fatigue accumulated throughout the day. Contrary to popular belief, getting enough sleep (around 7 hours) will not make you lazy or unproductive. Think of sleep as nature's built-in performance enhancer, allowing you to function at your best and experience lasting joy.

The Pursuit of Happiness

Effort and Individuality

The previous sections discussed some important factors that can contribute to a happy and contented life. While it is unrealistic to claim these factors will yield identical results for everyone, their effectiveness aligns directly with the effort you put into being happy.

Joy is a complex tapestry woven from many elements; focus on your strengths and let the rest fall into place. Remember, the fact that you are making a conscious effort to be happy signifies you are on the right path. So be yourself, follow some basic principles, and you will be able to walk tall with confidence.

Sensible Food and Nutrition

Balance and Moderation

Some foods are undeniably detrimental to your health, while others form the foundation of your diet. This does not mean eliminating all treats – an occasional pizza or pastry will not derail your progress. A little indulgence in chocolate or a slice of black forest cake will not cause weight gain or indigestion. In fact, delicious and satisfying food can contribute to mental well-being by fulfilling the body's needs. However, for most days, strive for a well-rounded diet incorporating recommended amounts of all essential nutrients. A balanced plate includes vegetables like carrots or broccoli alongside bacon – that is what we call sensible eating.

Avocation: Embracing Your Interests

An avocation is a leisure activity. Just as the body needs nourishment, the mind needs stimulation and relaxation. Knowing how to utilize your free time productively is key. Develop a hobby like reading, playing games, or listening to music – activities that bring you joy. Do not let anyone discourage you from pursuing your interests. Your free time belongs to you, and dedicating it to a hobby can enhance your focus and overall well-being.

9 WORKOUT TO WELLBEING

Engaging in activities that promote happiness and health is crucial for everyone. Physical activity is unrivaled in its ability to invigorate both the body and mind. Once you incorporate some form of exercise into your routine, you will likely experience greater relaxation and peace of mind.

Embrace the Activity You Enjoy

Choose a sport that ignites your passion, whether it is volleyball, swimming, or simply jogging. Some people find solitary gym sessions or jogs monotonous. To combat boredom, consider exercising with a friend or two, listening to your favorite music, or trying aerobics.

Explore and Experiment

You are more likely to enjoy activities you excel at, so explore different options and do not be afraid to experiment. Numerous clubs exist, catering to both specific interests and government initiatives. These can provide support and encouragement as you pursue a sport you enjoy. The moment you discover a talent, it fosters a sense of achievement, contributing significantly to your mental and physical well-being.

The Benefits of Exercise

Exercise ensures proper blood circulation throughout the body, promoting healthy digestion. It tones muscles, giving you a physique you can be proud of, and boosts your self-confidence. Even at rest, exercise helps burn calories. If you are over 30 and feel energized after a workout, do not be surprised – exercise can reverse the decline in metabolic rate.

Overall, Health and Well-being

Exercise combats various health issues, including lower back pain, abnormal blood pressure and sugar levels, and even colon cancer. It also promotes healthy HDL cholesterol levels. Maintaining good health is essential for enhancing happiness in your life. After all, there is no greater joy than feeling fit and healthy. Choose activities you enjoy – you will not regret it! Remember to complement your exercise routine with a balanced diet to avoid compromising your health. A healthy life truly is the key to a happy life!

10 **MANAGE STRESS**

Modern lifestyles bring a lot of stress in their wake. Combating this stress is crucial not only because it is harmful but also because it can lead to other psychological problems. Fortunately, fighting stress does not always require professional help. By following certain guidelines, we can manage stress effectively on our own.

Diet and Stress Management

Diet plays a significant role in stress management. Avoid the common pitfall of reaching for caffeine-rich beverages like coffee or soda. Instead, opt for water, fruit juices, and some fresh air. Limit your intake of excess fats, carbohydrates, sugars, and rich foods. If you are experiencing stress-related symptoms like anxiety, mood swings, or forgetfulness, incorporate a diet rich in fruits, vegetables, greens, nuts, and whole grains.

Exercise for Stress Relief

Physical exercise is a fantastic stress reliever in every sense of the word. Even in the office, where options might be limited, basic stretches and shrugs can release a lot of tension. A fitness instructor can teach you simple techniques you can use at your desk. Exercise can include conventional forms like aerobics, martial arts, or weightlifting. However, team sports like football or basketball can be equally effective. The social aspect of team sports can be highly motivating. The physical nature of exercise provides a safe outlet for pent-up stress, helping to regulate hormonal imbalances caused by stress. For immediate relief during sudden panic attacks, consider learning a few breathing exercises. Proper breathing is a key tool in combating stress.

Personalized Stress Release Techniques

Psychologists today encourage people to use personalized stress-release measures, no matter how unconventional they may seem. Techniques like popping bubble wrap, head-banging to heavy metal music, or even punching a bag can all be effective.

Declutter Your Environment

Whenever you feel stress mounting, the first step is to clear the clutter that often precedes it. This could mean tidying up your office desk, room, or kitchen. A well-organized workspace has a calming effect. Working in a cluttered environment can make things seem more out of control than they truly are.

Identify and Address the Root Cause

Finally, take a step back and consider your situation.

Try to identify the primary cause of your stress. Imagine how things would be different if you were stress-free. Most importantly, prioritize your life. Feeling overwhelmed by too many responsibilities can be a major stressor. Ask yourself: "Do I need a small raise, or do I need more time with my kids?" Pursue the option that will bring you greater happiness and well-being in the long run.

11 **THE IMPORTANCE OF RELAXATION**

Relaxation is an incredibly important part of life. When you are feeling energetic and motivated, relaxation might seem counterintuitive. However, both physically and mentally, it is crucial for optimizing your mental and physical resources. Relaxation methods vary from person to person. The key is to find what best calms your overactive mind and body, allowing you to experience a period of peaceful joy.

Relaxation: Not Inactivity

Relaxation does not equate to complete inactivity or succumbing to lethargy. On the contrary, it should be viewed to prepare yourself to pursue your dreams and passions with renewed vigor. Think of your body as a battery. Learning to relax and recharge allows it to function at its best.

Finding Your Relaxation Style

As mentioned earlier, different people find peace in different ways. For some, relaxation might surprisingly involve adrenaline-pumping activities like rock climbing or mountain trekking. They crave a break from routine by immersing themselves in nature, allowing them to unwind and revitalize.

Tailored Relaxation Techniques

Others might find relaxation in a quiet corner with a good book and headphones playing music. Still others might unwind by pursuing hobbies like writing, sketching, playing guitar, or even working on cars.

Regaining Perspective Through Relaxation

When we are intensely focused on achieving our goals, it is easy to lose perspective. We can become so fixated on reaching our destination that we lose sight of the bigger picture. Relaxation provides a chance to step back, take a break, and reassess our lives. By relaxing, we regain control and can redirect our energy and efforts in new, potentially more effective directions.

Preventing Burnout

Taking time off allows your body and mind the essential break they need to prevent burnout. It helps create a necessary creative distance, enabling you to step away from your work and analyze its strengths and weaknesses with a fresh perspective. So, the next time you feel neck pain from hunching over your computer, remember to take a deep breath and unwind!

12 **MEDITATIVE JOY**

Are you searching for something intangible, something that transcends the physical world? Then perhaps meditation can be of great help. Regardless of your religious beliefs, both prayer and meditation have a long history of promoting tranquility and stress relief.

The Benefits of Meditation

Meditation has been practiced for centuries to calm the mind, improve focus, and strengthen willpower.

The act of meditation itself is soothing, leaving you feeling refreshed afterward. It is known to improve blood circulation, nourishing all parts of your body. By relaxing your nerves, meditation can also contribute to glowing skin and overall health.

Creating a Meditation Practice

Establish a dedicated time for meditation in your daily routine. Consider mornings and evenings after bathing as ideal times.

To enhance your meditation experience, dim the lights, play soft instrumental music in the background, and use an air freshener to create a calming ambience. While meditating, you can either chant a prayer or visualize a peaceful scene, like a white lotus flower on a lake or a beautiful sunset.

The Power of Consistency

Practice meditation for 30 minutes each morning and evening to experience the profound sense of peace it can bring to your mind.

Meditation is a soulful and deeply relaxing practice that can also lead to self-discovery. Even on the busiest days, carving out time to meditate will yield noticeable benefits.

Meditation as a Family Activity

Consider making meditation a daily family ritual, gathering everyone to sit and meditate together at a specific time. After all, true happiness often stems from the happiness of those close to you. Inculcating this habit in children, particularly in today's fast-paced world, can significantly improve their well-being and performance in school and other aspects of life.

Inner Peace and Harmony

What greater joy can there be than experiencing peace and harmony in both mind and body? Meditation is rapidly gaining popularity worldwide as a powerful stress-reduction technique. In many religious places, professionals and devotees alike chant sacred hymns, allowing visitors and followers to experience the true essence of meditation.

Start Your Meditation Journey

Embrace meditation and witness the positive transformations it can bring to your life.

13 **MANAGING ANGER**

Taming the Anger Monster

In our increasingly stressful and intolerant world, anger seems to be the most common emotion people experience. Throughout a single day, we encounter a multitude of anger triggers – traffic jams, workplace disputes, endless lines. Even children get angry, at things like seemingly excessive homework or a pesky classmate.

The Why and How of Anger Management

It is crucial for everyone to learn to manage their anger. There are practical reasons to avoid letting anger control you. Anger affects us in significant and noticeable ways.

First and foremost, anger is inherently linked to unhappiness. Even a novice psychiatrist can recognize that a state of anger is unproductive. In fact, anger can lead to feelings of guilt, even for tasks we excel at. It also negatively impacts our relationships. By hindering communication, anger damages not only personal relationships (like marriages) but also social and professional ones. When we are angry, our social skills plummet. This negatively affects our current and potential work or business opportunities. This creates a vicious cycle – anger fuels stress, which in turn fuels more anger.

Strategies for Anger Management

Managing anger is a mark of maturity. It not only helps you deal with the immediate cause of anger but also increases your chances of achieving happiness in life. Controlling anger requires developing a system of emotional control mechanisms.

The first step is to avoid reacting impulsively. Carefully consider if getting angry is truly worth it. Does the cause of your anger matter in the long run? Will getting angry yield any positive consequences? It is also important to give the other person the benefit of the doubt – did they mean it maliciously, or have you done something similar in the past? Taking time to reflect often reduces anger levels. Even if it does not completely dissipate your anger, it can help you respond in a more measured way, minimizing self-inflicted harm. The classic method of counting to calm down can also be helpful.

Healthy Release Mechanisms

Finally, provide yourself with a healthy outlet for your anger. For example, if you feel the urge to yell at someone, go home and write down your frustrations on a piece of paper, then discard it. Engage in activities that help you release the negative emotions rather than letting them build up inside you.

14 **CONFLICT RESOLUTION**

Conflict: A Catalyst for Growth

Conflict is not inherently bad. When handled constructively, it can yield positive outcomes in any setting, be it at home, school, or the workplace. Conflict indicates that people are invested in what they are doing, which is a positive sign. The key to profiting from conflict lies in its resolution. Tackled effectively, conflict can foster understanding and compatibility, strengthening teams and families. It also prepares us for future collaborations by increasing self-awareness and understanding of others.

Prevention and Ground Rules

Before diving into conflict resolution, some key points deserve consideration. Prevention is always preferable to cure, so ideally, we should strive to avoid escalating situations. Even during disagreements, maintaining a cordial demeanor is crucial. Relationships require effort to build, and destroying them ultimately harms everyone. The focus should always be on the problem itself, not personal attacks. This involves giving the other party a fair hearing. Actively listen to their perspective, and ensure open communication. Only after establishing a foundation of facts should opinions come into play.

The Conflict Resolution Process

Conflict resolution starts with a shared understanding of the facts. The same information can have different interpretations for different people. Everyone's perspective is important and deserves to be voiced. Equally important is active listening from all parties involved – it is a two-way street at every stage.

Understanding the Impact

Next, discuss the various implications of the problem from each participant's viewpoint. Consider everyone's needs, interests, and concerns. Think about how the conflict hinders your performance, trust, or focus as a team or family.

Identifying the Core Issue and Solutions

These inputs should be used to pinpoint the specific problems everyone agrees upon. It might seem obvious, but disagreements often stem from differing perceptions of the core issue. Only then should everyone propose potential solutions.

Finding Common Ground

When choosing a solution, prioritize what benefits most people involved. Compromise is essential; achieving everything you want may not be possible.

However, by acting judiciously, you can certainly optimize the outcome for everyone.

15 **CLARITY & CONTENTMENT**

The Path to Enlightenment: A Mosaic of Moments
Enlightenment, like happiness, is a mosaic formed by
countless small yet fulfilling experiences throughout
life.

Living an Enlightened Life

An enlightened life is the life we all dream of – free
from worries, anxieties, and concerns. It is the ultimate
balance of detachment without isolation, and
individuality without selfishness. Like all positive
aspects of life, success and well-being are also crucial
components of an enlightened existence. While
success may be defined differently by each person,
based on personal choices, goals, and aspirations, the
truth remains that it ultimately stems from clear
thinking, abundant passion, and taking the right
actions.

Finding Passion in Everyday Life

You do not need lofty goals to prove your worth. True
value comes from pursuing your daily tasks with
passion, helping others around you, and loving what
you do. Developing a flexible personal plan while
embracing each day as it unfolds is an excellent
approach. This does not negate the importance of a
daily routine; however, your routine should not come

at the expense of your true interests and passions. For example, if you feel compelled to spend a day restoring your old car instead of going to the office, do it. These bursts of inspiration are rare, so make the most of them when they strike.

Acting on Your Passions

Passions and interests need to be translated into action. Loving to play guitar will not bring you closer to your dreams unless you share your music with others. Having a dream is just the beginning – hard work, dedication, perseverance, and focus are essential to turn it into reality. If building a stamp collection is your dream, start collecting stamps today.

Continuous Growth and Connection

Always be on the lookout for new opportunities to hone and improve your skills. If you are a skilled martial artist, seek out others who share your passion and understand your dedication.

Clarity and the Journey of Self-Improvement

Constant self-improvement requires clarity in thought and action. Living with this approach will minimize regrets, and even your failures will be testaments to your earnest efforts.

16 SCIENCE OF HAPPINESS

The Many Paths to Happiness and Success

Everyone deserves to be happy and content in life, regardless of their background. Happiness is a personal journey, and what brings joy to one person may not resonate with another. Some individuals find fulfillment in workaholic dedication, pouring endless hours into perfecting a project. Others chase financial success, while still others discover happiness in hobbies or leisure activities. The key is to identify what truly brings you joy and fulfillment.

Success: A Personal Definition

Success is subjective and unique to everyone.

Facing Your Fear of Failure

Before setting goals for success, consider your motivations. Fear of failure, although seemingly negative, can be a healthy motivator. It can push you to appreciate the value of success. However, the key is to learn bravery and confront the possibility of failure head-on, rather than avoiding it altogether.

Finding Intrinsic Motivation

Success driven by external validation, such as proving

yourself to others, holds little meaning. True satisfaction comes from achieving success for yourself, for the inherent joy and fulfillment it brings. While your loved ones may derive happiness from your achievements, their ultimate desire is your happiness. By pursuing your passions, emotions, and aspirations, the entire process – the effort, dedication, and accomplishment – becomes a source of immense satisfaction.

Money and Happiness: Not Always Synonymous

Money is certainly important. It can provide a comfortable lifestyle, but it should never be the sole motivator or sole measure of success. Happiness is a state of mind, not a reflection of material possessions. Focus on what truly motivates you, what ignites your drive and passion. The material rewards, like a fancy car or a spacious apartment, may naturally follow because of your dedication and pursuit of your true passions.

17 **FACE YOUR FEARS**

Conquering Fear: The Key to Success

Old proverbs warn that a person without fear is a person without talents or abilities. We naturally tend to fear loss: loss of power, individuality, status, or loved ones. Fear is a common response to the unforeseen changes life throws our way. However, to achieve success, you must learn to manage your fears through positive thoughts and actions. But first, you need to identify them before you can battle them.

The Root of Fear: Insecurity

The fundamental fears that hinder success often stem from insecurities. Overcoming one fear empowers you to tackle others, creating a snowball effect of courage.

Understanding Your Fears: The Fear of Poverty

Fear of failure and financial loss can prevent you from giving your all to a project. While financial security is important for you and your family, do not be discouraged by setbacks. You can tighten your belt and find ways to save. Remember, even legendary Microsoft was founded by Bill Gates, a young college dropout, working on a shoestring budget. Trust in your abilities and resourcefulness to overcome challenges.

Fear of Criticism: A Tool for Growth

Criticism, particularly constructive criticism, is valuable. It helps you identify flaws and areas for improvement. Do not be disheartened if your initial effort receives criticism. Often, the critique is not about your effort or passion, but about minor oversights or glitches. Learning to accept criticism helps you mature through practical trial and error.

Fear of Physical Breakdown: A Catalyst for Action

Fear of illness hindering your dreams can be turned into a motivator. Use it as an excuse to prioritize your health. Hit the gym regularly or partake in an hour of daily exercise. View physical activity as a reward for your body, helping you achieve your goals. A strong and healthy body leads to a stress-free, active mind.

18 EMBRACE THE UNKNOWN

Conquering Fear: The Power of Positive Action

As discussed earlier, most fears stem from real insecurities and anxieties. We anticipate limitations before they even arise. The most effective weapon against them is the power of positive thought and action. However, to leverage this power, you first need to identify the source of your fear and how it affects you.

Fear of Losing Passion: Reigniting the Flame

Do you worry that years down the line, you will lose interest or drive in your current project? Is a fear of fading passion holding you back? If so, you may have lost focus. Reexamine why this project is important to you and those you love. Rediscovering its relevance will reignite your interest and reassure you of your passion. If you truly love what you do, you will give it your all to see it succeed. Think positively and do not let minor insecurities extinguish your love.

Fear of Negativity: Embracing Patience and Persistence

When you have poured hard work, spontaneous effort, and genuine passion into a project, you naturally want to shield it from negativity and pessimism. Patience is key here. You must be strong enough to wait for your project to mature. Positive thoughts and actions leave no room for pessimistic doubts about its success. Legendary American industrialist Henry Ford never lost hope or succumbed to bitterness when his prototypes failed. He fought relentlessly to preserve his dream, ultimately becoming a household name in the Western world.

Fear of Oblivion: Finding Fulfillment in the Present

Everything on Earth succumbs to time. You may not live long enough to see your passion become a widely shared inspiration. However, we live in the present, and so should you. If your love and dedication bring you peace of mind and pride in your work, that is enough to feel joy. If your passion is sincere, your work will likely gain recognition and appreciation.

19 **BOUNCING BACK**

Failure: A Stepping Stone to Success

For many, failure and loss are sensitive topics. Naturally, we do not embark on endeavors expecting or even considering failure. Phrases like "failure is part of the game" or "participation is more important than winning" may sound good in theory, but offer little comfort to someone who poured their heart into something and fell short.

It is true that setbacks are the foundation of every success story, but our minds need to be prepared to handle them – initial failures, disappointments, and the emotional toll they take. "Training to fail" might seem counterintuitive at first, but it is a growing trend in human resource management across multinational corporations.

We all know the story of Robert the Bruce, who learned perseverance after watching a spider's repeated attempts to spin its web. This parable is a testament to the importance of never giving up. However, it is also an early example of witnessing the mind's restorative power in action.

After a setback, it is natural to feel disoriented and even lose direction. This is when the mind goes into introspection mode, analyzing what went wrong. It is an intensive process as the mind confronts uncomfortable questions about its weaknesses and shortcomings. However, it is crucial to stay focused and not lose sight of our overarching goals during this self-evaluation. The mind needs to be trained to regroup, recover, and re-energize after a setback.

Avoiding the outcome by burying yourself in a busy schedule is not productive. It merely delays the inevitable confrontation with uncomfortable truths. You need to be brave enough to acknowledge your flaws and determined enough to learn from your mistakes.

Self-help experts often say that a wounded mind can be surprisingly receptive. Failure strips away mental clutter – unrealistic expectations, self-satisfaction, complacency, and dangerous overconfidence. The mind becomes a blank slate, ready to absorb new information without preconceptions or hasty judgments. In the wake of failure, what is needed is calm acceptance of events and a period of rest and reflection.

20 **FAILURE TEACHES SUCCESS**

Failure: The Crucible of Success

Failure is an inevitable part of our daily lives. Every attempt we make, every journey we embark on, carries the possibility of a setback. Acknowledging this possibility is what pushes us to give our best effort. Setbacks are like our personal trial by fire, the hardships that strengthen our resolve. As the saying goes, "He who handles failure well knows how to handle success." Without resorting to philosophical complexities, it is safe to say that learning from failure is essential for success in life.

We are all individuals with different lifestyles and approaches to life. Naturally, our perceptions of failure will also differ. While we should not be paralyzed by the fear of failure, having a backup plan – a "Plan B" – demonstrates mature thinking. Developing a contingency plan for when your primary strategy falters shows not only that you accept failure as a possibility, but also that you are determined to overcome it.

Some react to failure with extremes, resorting to self-criticism and anger. If the failure stemmed from your own mistakes, lashing out will not salvage the situation. It will only deplete your self-confidence and lead to abandoning your projects. True passion requires full commitment to the cause. When faced with a setback, take a step back and calmly analyze the factors that led to failure.

For others, a complete break works best. Completely disconnecting from the situation may help you regain focus. Use this time for self-discovery and self-appreciation. Reconnect with life's simple pleasures – listen to some Bach, or pick up a new hobby. Spending quality time with loved ones can also work wonders in reviving your spirit.

21 **PRIORITIZE**

Setting and Achieving Goals: A Roadmap to Success

Objectives, or goals, are essential tools for measuring our progress. We need a yardstick to accurately evaluate our strengths, weaknesses, passions, and vulnerabilities. These yardsticks are not imposed externally; we create them ourselves. This is where setting goals comes in. Whenever we aspire to complete a project, express our talents, or pursue our passions, we are unconsciously setting goals for ourselves. Successfully completing projects fulfills our commitment to these goals and paves the way for setting new ones. Goals act like stepping stones, leading you towards a fulfilling life.

However, it is important not to be overwhelmed by goals. Personal goals and objectives are meant for guidance and self-evaluation, helping you progress steadily. A good practice is to regularly review, reset, and re-implement these goals to stay on track. For instance, you might set a year-end goal of buying a car. Before diving in, break this goal down into smaller, achievable milestones. This could involve creating a plan for installments or spreading the car's cost over time. Treat these smaller objectives as personal milestones, and you will be surprised how much closer your final goal seems.

Throughout this process, appreciate your worth and effort. Setting goals requires significant passion, thought, and dedication. As you complete smaller objectives, reward yourself with a celebratory outing or a long-desired purchase. These occasional rewards will fuel your efforts, serving as a substitute for the ultimate fulfillment of your larger goal.

Finally, do not indefinitely postpone your goals. Setting a specific timeframe for completing your objectives instills a sense of urgency and accountability. For example, if you designate a specific date to start going to the gym, honor that commitment. By planning your goals and objectives in advance, you increase your chances of successfully achieving your dreams and pursuing your passions.

22 **DO IT NOW**

Seize the Moment: Making Every Second Count

We often hear people say, "I'm waiting for the right time." However, the "right time" may never come. Every moment can be your golden opportunity. You never know when fortune will strike, so constant preparation is key. The concept of seizing every opportunity predates even the English language, and people around the world continue to find new ways to leverage every moment.

"Opportunity" is a broad term. It could be the perfect moment to launch a project, the right gut feeling to walk away from a situation, or a time to increase personal effort. To capitalize on opportunities, first ask yourself: "Am I ready to seize this moment?" Your answer will determine your level of preparation. Opportunity is life's reward for sustained passion and effort. Wasting it undermines your commitment and ambitions.

Opportunity empowers you to choose between needs and desires. Imagine having a dollar to spend. The world is your oyster! With self-control, you decide between equally tempting options: saving it, investing it, or buying a lottery ticket. Identify your passions and natural inclinations. If you are confident, creative, and willing to take risks, that dollar could be the opportunity of a lifetime. Who knows, you might turn it into a million-dollar business!

Preparing for opportunity is not difficult – just put in some honest effort. Know exactly what you would do if given the chance to showcase yourself. Have your ideas and defenses ready.

On the practical side, be prepared to step outside your comfort zone. If you truly believe you have what it takes to succeed, be willing to sacrifice luxuries, preconceived notions, and limiting beliefs. Self-confidence is crucial. It helps you define your aspirations and act.

23 CONQUER CHALLENGES

Confronting Challenges: Stepping Stones to Success

Any endeavor you undertake will inevitably encounter obstacles and limitations. Prudence lies not in ignoring them, but in confronting them head-on. Proposing something new or creating something original will always involve hurdles. The key is to stay calm and focused, not to get discouraged by these challenges. A little focus and patience can make a world of difference.

The Challenge of Supportive Skeptics

Family, friends, and colleagues are often the people whose opinions matter most to us. Ironically, these very support structures can also become obstacles, hindering the pursuit of your passions. Handle these situations with sensitivity to avoid causing offense. Typically, their concerns stem from good intentions. They might question your passion, deeming it impractical, unrewarding, or even risky. For instance, they might resist your desire to switch careers from banking to become a scuba instructor, despite your enthusiasm. Perseverance and focus are key. Your hard work and dedication will eventually convince them of your sincerity.

The Financial Hurdle

Money, a universal concern, can be a significant barrier to success. Financial limitations often deter us from pursuing passions, interests, or lifelong dreams. For example, money might have prevented you from attending your preferred university or forced you to abandon a project due to lack of funding.

If your project is fueled by passion, find ways to make the money yourself. Be prepared to make sacrifices, prioritizing your passion over certain worldly comforts. Starting your project on a smaller scale can attract potential investors or financiers. Persuasiveness, creativity, and earnestness will ensure your dreams do not die due to a lack of funds.

24 MANEUVER THROUGH

Overcoming Obstacles: A Journey of Patience and Strategy

As discussed earlier, encountering obstacles does not necessitate a forceful approach. Instead, patience and strategy are key. Learning to navigate these hurdles effectively prepares you to confront your limitations. However, before tackling them, you need to identify the obstacles in your immediate environment. You would be surprised how often seemingly insignificant obstacles can stifle your ambitions and passions.

The Challenge of Time Management

Time is of the essence when pursuing your ambitions. It determines whether you have the energy and dedication required. People often cite lack of time as an excuse for unfinished projects or failed attempts. Our busy lifestyles often force us to work late or prioritize family and friends. However, remember that your time belongs to you, and you have the right to allocate it strategically.

Consider waking up a little earlier each day. This not only benefits your health but also gives you a head start on your schedule. During lunch breaks, opt for easily consumed meals to finish quickly and return to work or your project ten minutes early. On your commute home, prioritize speed over comfort. Utilize this reclaimed time to pursue your passions, plan your projects, or simply relax and recharge.

Finding Career Satisfaction

The ideal career is not solely about money; it is about achieving a balance between income and job satisfaction. Invest your efforts in a career that brings you pride, fulfillment, and a positive work environment. A job that fosters your creativity and individuality will empower you to excel and set new personal bests.

25 **COURAGE GAINS**

Finding Courage in the Face of Tragedy

Imagine experiencing a terrible accident at the young age of 25, losing your parents, two brothers, and your unborn baby girl in your eighth month of pregnancy. Just imagining this scenario is distressing. Surely, you would not wish this on even your worst enemy.

Annie Oakland, from Laguna Beach, California, unfortunately experienced this unimaginable loss. At 25, the pain and anguish must have been overwhelming. She could have easily succumbed to despair, letting it define her life. Instead, she asked herself a powerful question: Is this what her loved ones would have wanted for her? The answer, undoubtedly, was no. They would have wanted her to live a life filled with courage, inspiring others, and finding happiness. Today, Annie lives with her husband, who provided strength and support throughout her journey.

Perhaps you have encountered similar stories throughout your life. We've all seen movies that move us deeply and witnessed acts of courage in those around us. Life, though fundamentally simple, can be complicated by unexpected tragedies. These difficult circumstances demand that we draw upon the lessons of courage we have learned from past experiences and stories. Challenges that shake us and force us to break free from old patterns can ultimately be transformative.

Courage has many definitions around the world. But to navigate the joys and sorrows of life, we all need a certain measure of it. Think of courage as a persistent child tugging at your pants, demanding your immediate attention. It is an urgent call to action, something you cannot ignore.

Do not let unforeseen tragedies defeat you. Let courage be your magic brush, washing away sadness and painting your life with the vibrant colors of joy.

26 **THE POWER OF SINCERITY**

Commitment: The Fuel for Passion and Purpose

Throughout our lives, we take on numerous tasks without considering our ability to see them through. Often, our passions are intertwined with our dreams, direction, and motivations, making it difficult to resist their call and commit. However, once we commit to a task, someone else's project, or even a chosen way of life, it becomes our ethical and moral responsibility to persevere. Countless endeavors and dreams have crumbled due to a lack of motivation and dedication from those undertaking them.

Before diving into something that piques your interest, consider a few things:

How will it contribute to my growth?

A genuine interest, passion, or constructive hobby aims to make you a better, more focused, and committed individual. For example, a passion for reading expands your creative horizons, ignites your imagination, and strengthens your ability to express yourself. When you deeply care about something, you will find it easier to focus your efforts on doing what you love. Hobbies and interests instill discipline and order in our lives by making us accountable for completing these tasks. If your new area of interest lacks a deeper purpose, your initial excitement might fade, and you will lose momentum.

Motivation Matters

Motivation is another crucial factor in fostering dedication and passion. People define and find motivation differently. Some are driven by external incentives, while others are fueled by the joy and satisfaction that comes with commitment and participation. For the latter, the process itself, with its inherent joy and self-satisfaction, is paramount. It is up to each of us to identify the specific factor that motivates us in any endeavor. Once you discover what truly motivates you, finding it within your chosen pursuits will not be as difficult.

Effective Time Management

Now that you have identified your key motivators and personal interests, it is time to manage your schedule effectively. If you decide to take on a new commitment, ensure it does not add undue stress to your existing activities.

27 **PUSH PAST LIMITS, DAILY**

Conquering Your Limits: The Road to Success

We often shy away from jobs, prospects, or responsibilities due to perceived limitations. These limitations often stem from a lack of conviction, courage, planning, determination, or inspiration. Uncompleted or abandoned projects can later lead to feelings of heartbreak, regret, and disappointment. A mind burdened by these limitations starts to view them as natural and ingrained habits. To achieve success, you must confront these psychological roadblocks and learn to overcome them.

By regularly challenging yourself to push past your perceived limitations, you can turn exceeding them into a habit.

Know Your Boundaries

Understanding the true nature of your limitations is crucial for effectively confronting them. Whenever you experience a loss of confidence or hesitation, ask yourself: What specific concerns are holding me back? Is it a lack of money, fear of failure, or a deficiency in courage? Once you identify your limitations, you can use them as benchmarks to measure your progress. For example, weight trainers often start with weights at their maximum limit. Once they have adapted to this level of effort, lifting lighter weights becomes comparatively easier.

Defeating Your Limitations: Your Allies in Success

To conquer your limitations, you need to identify your allies. Your greatest allies in achieving success are self-belief, confidence in your abilities, talent, and a strong sense of curiosity. We have discussed the first three in detail, so let us explore curiosity. Curiosity is a healthy amount of interest, mixed with anticipation, to gain knowledge. It is a crucial positive quality, as it helps us adopt new perspectives. Curiosity aligns with our natural instincts for discovery and knowledge seeking, and is considered the primary way we learn. Healthy curiosity opens the mind to new ideas and perspectives, broadening our horizons and fostering a more open-minded approach. Curiosity fueled Fleming's discovery of penicillin, Madame Curie's discovery of radium, and Columbus's discovery of North America. Embrace curiosity and inquisitiveness, because success often favors those who dare to explore beyond the familiar.

28 **UNLOCK JOY**

Joy: A Fleeting but Cultivable Treasure

Joy, a precious yet elusive feeling, requires effort to cultivate but can easily slip away. Throughout history, humankind has sought to define and quantify joy by factors like wealth, health, and relationships. However, happiness is not a bottled elixir concocted with the right ingredients. Joy, often triggered by seemingly ordinary things like a breathtaking view, a peaceful moment, or a minor accomplishment, is truly a fleeting experience.

Personal Paths to Happiness

Happiness is a deeply personal concept, defying universal trends or formulas. People find joy by pursuing their passions and unique life philosophies. For some, security and financial stability bring joy. Others find it in fulfilling relationships, fostering the well-being of loved ones, or even accumulating wealth. Ironically, immense wealth and success do not guarantee happiness, as some highly successful individuals grapple with personal anxieties and insecurities. Conversely, someone working tirelessly can still experience joy.

The Elusive Definition of Happiness

The age-old question of "what truly makes us happy?" has fueled endless searches for happiness secrets. While happiness itself might be indefinable, the path to achieving it is not. Happiness might involve compromise or sacrifice, where you prioritize the well-being of others over personal desires, yet find joy in those selfless acts. Contentment with your life is a strong indicator that you are on the right track to happiness and inner peace.

Choosing Happiness

Some individuals seem naturally optimistic, lacking insecurities and anxieties. But the factors leading to contentment and joy are largely within your control. It is empowering to realize that happiness is a choice. Confidence is key to living a joyful life, allowing you to embrace your feelings without apology or arrogance. If your intuition guides you towards a project that sparks joy, pride, and a sense of purpose, do not let external pressures hold you back.

29 **LIVING WELL DEFINED**

The Art of Cultivating Happiness: Mastering the Elements of Everyday Life

The perfect life, an elusive ideal, often remains just out of reach. To find the essence of happiness, we must learn to control and manage certain key factors in our lives. These factors can be broadly categorized as positive, contributing to a sense of well-being, or negative, hindering a healthy and fulfilling life. By regulating these common factors to our advantage, we gain a degree of control over our own happiness. The goal is to cultivate an overall appreciation for the regularity and significance of these elements within your life. You will need to limit some factors, enhance others, and find a balance for the rest to ensure a well-coordinated and intelligent approach to modern living.

Essential Elements for a Fulfilling Life

Here are some key factors to consider in your daily life:

Domestic Harmony: The Foundation of Happiness

Peace and harmony at home are fundamental prerequisites for true happiness. A calm, serene, and supportive home environment fosters personal effort and creativity. Conversely, a bitter, tense atmosphere characterized by rigid power structures and strained family relationships jeopardizes creativity. This kind of environment is detrimental to starting new ventures and cultivating hobbies and interests, as it offers minimal peace of mind. Ensure you have a positive home environment that allows you to function effectively and contribute to its continued well-being. Furthermore, eliminate any instances of domestic abuse or violence. Similarly, do not allow moments of tragedy or grief to linger, as this can create a stagnant and oppressive atmosphere.

Family Support: Strengthening the Bonds

Address any family emergencies promptly. Support among family members strengthens familial bonds and fosters trust and harmony within the household. Simply letting your loved ones know you are there for them demonstrates your importance as a family member.

Education and Career: Investing in Your Future

Do not let financial burdens hinder your academic career or divert you from your desired career path. Be prepared to make compromises and sacrifices to pursue the education you desire and secure a profession that aligns with your passions.

30 **FOREVER FAMILY**

The Rejuvenating Power of Family

Feeling overwhelmed by work? Easily frustrated and irritable? Spending quality time with loved ones can be a powerful remedy. Reconnecting with family reminds you that life extends beyond the workplace. Family bonds are an indescribable treasure. The simple act of sitting and talking with those you love and care for provides the energy and spirit to tackle life's challenges.

Everyone faces problems, and solutions are unique to each situation. However, one of the most effective paths to happiness is finding love. As Vincent Van Gogh aptly said, "Love is eternal. The aspect may change, but the essence remains." Love manifests in various forms. Whether it is a weekend family getaway, visiting grandparents, or watching your daughter learn to ride a bike, each experience holds its own special value. Each family relationship offers a unique blend of emotional connection and fulfillment.

From your two-year-old son's first crawl to your partner's return from a long workday to your mother's quiet enjoyment of gardening, everyone experiences a special kind of happiness when you choose to spend time with them, making them feel loved and valued. This love, in turn, uplifts you and relieves stress. It helps you rediscover joy in your work and life in general.

The beauty of family ties is that no single relationship can replace another. Each bond is special and irreplaceable, offering a unique connection. The presence of loved ones, especially during difficult times, is a source of immense comfort and joy. When life seems pointless, friends and family remind you of your worth. The best part? They give unconditionally and welcome you with open arms whenever you seek their company.

So, go ahead! Make time for your loved ones and embrace a life filled with joy and connection.

31 MINDFUL MOMENTS

Reclaiming Your Happy Place: Rekindling the Power of Past Achievements

We often find ourselves reminiscing about the best days of our lives, yearning to relive the ecstasy of happiness, success, and satisfaction with our efforts. These experiences need not be extraordinary feats requiring superhuman effort. Few of us have scaled the peaks of glory and universal admiration.

A seemingly ordinary experience, like achieving first place in class, playing your first guitar solo, or writing your first poem, can leave an indelible mark on your memory. The key lies in using these memories to build your confidence and belief in your abilities. Reflect on your life and identify those special moments you wish you could relive every day. You will likely find that these were times when you felt happiest, like a chosen one destined for success.

Believe it or not, these moments were not solely the result of fortunate circumstances, but rather the blossoming of your inherent talents and abilities. During your happiest times, you likely leveraged your intrinsic skills subconsciously, achieving a remarkable level of control and mastery. To cultivate more of these "perfect days," you need to respect your own abilities. It does not matter if they seem insignificant compared to someone else's expertise. Simply taking joy in what you do best and diligently pursuing it is enough to make your day.

The most important thing is to never give up on your dreams. While you may not be that wild-haired college kid anymore, that spirit still resides within you. Never relinquish your dreams and passions, for they are the essence of who you are. Modern proponents of healthy living consistently emphasize the importance of dreams and aspirations as building blocks of character.

Once you discover your niche area of expertise, you will likely pour your heart and soul into making it a success. When you love what you do, the mental barriers formed by fear, hatred, anxiety, and self-doubt crumble away. With time, conviction, and confidence, you will not only discover your calling but also use it as a stepping stone to your dreams.

32 **FAMILY MATTERS**

The Enduring Importance of Family Activities in Modern Society

In today's modern, nuclear family structure, family activities are more important than ever. The family unit serves as the foundation of society, and the lessons learned within this core group have lasting repercussions on how individuals interact with the larger world. As humans become increasingly isolated, a corresponding rise in selfishness is observed. To counteract this trend, fostering teamwork is essential. Family activities provide a valuable microcosm to illustrate how teamwork benefits everyone.

We often underestimate the power of simple activities to become cherished family rituals that strengthen bonds. A family picnic, a board game night, or even a movie night together can teach valuable lessons in cooperation, generosity, and compromise. These seemingly mundane experiences unknowingly equip us with vital skills for navigating the world outside the home, whether in the workplace, on the playground, or at social gatherings. Individuals who have strong family values instilled through conscious and unconscious family rituals tend to perform better because teamwork, understanding, and flexibility become second nature.

The world is truly shrinking into a global village. In our daily interactions, we encounter a much broader ethnic, economic, and religious cross-section of people than previous generations. Consequently, the need for tolerance and camaraderie is greater than ever. Family rituals play a crucial role in fostering these qualities by bringing people together in a shared space. Communication is the cornerstone of survival in a multicultural world, and there is no better teacher than fundamental family interaction.

As mentioned earlier, these activities need not be elaborate. A shared meal or simply watching a game together on television can be effective. Families can also develop their own unique rituals, such as engaging in a specific activity on a particular holiday. Holidays offer a prime opportunity to strengthen familial bonds. Historically, all cultures have incorporated small customs that promote unity, humility, and working as part of a system. For example, in many parts of Asia and Africa, the tradition of seeking blessings from elders before embarking on a journey or undertaking a new venture is still practiced.

The adage that "all education begins at home" holds true. While celebrating holidays with family or cheering for your favorite team together may seem like mere entertainment, these experiences are instrumental in preparing you for the world beyond the home.

33 **PRIORITIZE YOURSELF**

The Power of Constructive Selfishness: Embracing Your Dreams

Do not be surprised by this chapter's topic: constructive selfishness. We will be discussing a different kind of selfishness than the destructive kind we often hear about.

There comes a time in life when you need to prioritize yourself to fulfill your ambitions and discover your purpose. This does not mean becoming self-absorbed; instead, it is about becoming self-centered enough to stop letting your fears and doubts hold you back.

"Selfish" may have negative connotations, but here, let us consider it a powerful tool for personal growth, ultimately enabling you to give more of yourself to the world. This requires challenging societal norms that may initially seem counterintuitive.

Imagine your lifelong dream is to own a specific bike. You have the means to buy it, but your parents, fearing an accident, forbid it. In this case, prioritizing your passion and following your dream necessitates putting your own needs first – that's constructive selfishness in action.

It is crucial to distinguish "selfishness" from "greed."

Seeking selfish pleasure at the expense of others' well-being, mistreatment, or constant self-sacrifice is nothing but greed. Indulgence and greed are always destructive. True joy should never come at the cost of another's sorrow. Be selfish, but be yourself so you can authentically share your full potential with the world.

By neglecting a healthy sense of constructive self-centeredness, you allow external forces to dictate your desires. The world inevitably influences us, but constantly sacrificing your own desires to fulfill the expectations of others stifles your soul. Remember, you are here to spread kindness in your own unique way, while pursuing your own joy. Self-acceptance should be the fundamental rhythm of your life, which embodies constructive selfishness.

Think of yourself as a plant struggling to flourish in weed-infested soil. The external factors are the weeds. To truly thrive, you must remove them and create space for your own growth. Distance yourself from attitudes, people, beliefs, or activities that do not bring you joy and fulfillment. This requires embracing constructive selfishness!

34 **NO BLAME GAME**

The Art of Lasting Joy in Relationships

We all enter relationships with the hope of finding happiness. We believe the person we choose is the perfect match. Love, support, companionship, and admiration from your partner can transform your world. Naturally, both partners have desires and expectations of each other. When these are met, happiness in the relationship seems assured.

However, within the comfort of a happy relationship, some crucial aspects of human nature can be easily forgotten. We neglect the reality that our partner may not always be able to fulfill our every wish. Even minor unmet expectations can lead to disappointment and resentment. We start blaming our partner, forgetting all the past joys shared together.

Happiness in a relationship is, by nature, transient. It ebbs and flows. A shift in perspective is necessary. Your happiness should not hinge on unfulfilled desires and demands. True joy is different. It is an attitude that can be cultivated and nurtured, much like the transformation of a newborn baby who needs constant care into a self-sufficient adult.

It is tempting to nag your loved one about disappointments. We blame our partner for our own frustrations or workplace woes. This is a recipe for destroying joy. Your partner has the right to experience their own emotions. If you are unhappy, it is your responsibility to find healthy ways to cope – it does not necessarily reflect poorly on your partner. Remember, you are not their judge or jury.

A famous saying captures the essence of joy perfectly: "When we are kids, we play with toys. When we mature, we seek the genuine thing." And that genuine thing is joy. The joy of life develops gradually and stems from our actions and choices.

35 **KINDNESS WINS**

The Enduring Joy of Giving

There is no greater joy in life than spreading love and helping those in need. Countless unfortunate souls exist, including orphaned children living on the streets or in orphanages. If you have some time, money, or spare clothes to donate, and want to experience the joy of giving and sharing, there are many opportunities. You could help the child begging on the sidewalk on your way to work, or support an orphanage that raises funds through cultural events.

Humans are naturally social creatures with inherent kindness. Most people extend a helping hand when they can, as it brings a unique sense of fulfillment. Recognition and respect often follow acts of charity. As the saying goes, "Shared sorrow is lessened, shared joy is increased." Charity is not the only path to joy. Leftover food from a party or an extra cake you baked can be shared, bringing a smile to someone's face.

Sharing does not have to be material. You can spread joy by getting involved. For example, if the orphanage across the street is rehearsing a play, you could participate by acting, providing refreshments, or simply applauding their efforts. After all, time is a precious gift.

Charitable work allows you to positively impact the lives of others. Ultimately, we all desire love and respect for who we are. What purpose does a life devoid of service to humanity hold? Go forth, spread joy, and discover the true pleasure of giving and loving.

36 **NATURE'S BLISS**

The Joy of Gardening: Cultivating Beauty, Peace, and Well-being

One of the most rewarding paths to joy is pursuing a solitary activity that enhances nature's beauty and serenity. What embodies beauty and peace more than nature itself? Gardening offers a perfect hobby, allowing you to connect with nature while fostering your own sense of well-being.

Plants and flowers are surprisingly adaptable. You can cultivate small plants in containers on your balcony or even indoors, although natural sunlight is ideal for optimal photosynthesis. If you have a backyard, consider expanding your gardening endeavors. You can cultivate a diverse array of ornamental plants, flowers, and even fruit trees. While the flowers and ornamentals beautify your surroundings and uplift your spirit, the vegetables can become a delightful addition to your homegrown kitchen bounty.

The act of growing plants not only fosters a sense of accomplishment from creating something new but also benefits the environment in this age of pollution and climate change. Gardens often attract a cheerful group of children. If you choose to open your garden to visitors, you will be rewarded with the heartwarming sight of children of all ages, as beautiful as the flowers themselves, frolicking in your green haven. Furthermore, planting trees and greenery around your home naturally purifies the air you breathe, contributing to your overall health.

Gardening can be as intricate or casual as you desire. The beauty lies in the fact that casual gardening requires minimal investment. With just a few seeds, some basic fertilizer, and a trusty shovel, you are all set to begin your gardening adventure.

A little initial patience is all it takes in gardening. Witnessing the fruits (or vegetables!) of your labor will undoubtedly bring immense satisfaction. If you yearn to take it beyond a hobby, you can always expand your garden. The sense of pride in your flourishing creation and the tranquil space it provides for relaxation are unparalleled joys.

37 **MAKE A PET PAL**

The Joy of Pets: Filling Your Life with Furry (or Feathered) Friends

Do you return to an empty home, feeling discouraged and lacking something to look forward to? Are you an older couple seeking companionship, or perhaps you have small children yearning for a furry friend? If so, adopting a pet could be the transformative answer you have been searching for.

Animals bring joy and companionship. Their loyalty is unwavering, offering unconditional love even when the world seems cold. While caring for a pet can be a significant time commitment, the rewards are immeasurable. Imagine returning home after a long day to the enthusiastic greeting and cuddly embrace of your furry companion. Even on days spent indoors, most pets enjoy your company, creating a sense of connection and belonging.

While dogs often come to mind first, there is a vast array of adorable animals to consider, from independent cats to playful rabbits and energetic hamsters. Choosing the right pet depends on your personality and lifestyle. Active individuals living in the countryside might find a horse to be the perfect match. Even birds and fish can provide entertainment and companionship for some.

If you question the positive impact a pet can have on your life, consider the heartwarming gaze of a puppy during feeding time, or the soothing purr of a contented cat as you stroke its fur. The bond you form is profound and meaningful.

Whether you are single or a family seeking a spark of joy, pets can enrich your lives in countless ways. From taking your dog for a walk or riding your horse across open fields, to playing with fish or simply listening to birdsong, pet ownership offers a world of excitement and connection. Embrace this opportunity and discover a newfound sense of purpose and companionship, perhaps revealing aspects of yourself you never knew existed.

38 **DEVOTIONAL DELIGHT**

Finding Joyful Devotion: A Celebration of Faith

We turn to God in times of joy and sorrow. In moments of despair, we may even seek solace in worship until happiness returns. Some individuals find constant joy in worshipping the Almighty, in good times and bad. This unwavering, joyful devotion is precisely what God desires from his followers. As Saint Augustine described God's nature, "He is a circle whose center is everywhere and its circumference nowhere." Make a joyful sound to the Almighty, and he welcomes you with the happiness you deserve.

However, true, and joyful worship is selfless. We must examine ourselves during times of contentment and accomplishment. Some may sing, dance, laugh, or giggle constantly, forgetting to express gratitude to God. Conversely, they may curse the Lord when faced with hardship. It is crucial to remember that devotion should stem from both mind and heart. We should not approach God's presence solely to seek personal gain.

You may encounter individuals who appear deeply engrossed in fervent prayer, seemingly expecting worldly conquest without effort. Isn't such a mindset illogical? Friends, success, and joy are two sides of the same coin, not rewards attainable solely through prayer. One must dedicate consistent effort to reap the rewards of hard work. As the saying goes, "you reap what you sow." If you strive to be a millionaire, you may very well achieve that goal. However, the key to reaching that status lies in persistent action, with God's blessings following as a result.

Reverend D. Martyn Lloyd-Jones offered a profound definition of worship: "Worship means the heart going out in fervent praise and adoration to God." Essentially, Lloyd-Jones suggests that true worship is not the mechanical repetition of prayers. Rather, it is the outpouring of your heart in fervent reverence for God. In return, you may receive blessings of happiness and peace.

39 UNEARTH YOUR SPARK

Finding Joy and Excitement Within Your Routine

While establishing a routine is undeniably beneficial, the comfort and predictability it brings can sometimes lead to a sense of stagnancy. Sticking solely to routine can inadvertently sacrifice excitement and zest for a false sense of security. Boredom creeps in, making your life monotonous and diminishing your enthusiasm for your work. While drastic measures like quitting your job for momentary satisfaction might be impulsive, there are ways to inject a spark of excitement into your routine. Remember, the key ingredient to happiness is actively seeking out joy and fulfillment within your current lifestyle. Striking a balance between joy, passion, and excitement can significantly enhance your efforts and achievements.

The Importance of Excitement

Daily work fatigue often stems from mental exhaustion. When you feel you have no new ideas to contribute, your efforts become disillusioning. Break the cycle of monotony by introducing fresh approaches and initiatives in the workplace. Suggest new projects, embrace professional challenges, and welcome opportunities to learn and grow. The thrill of venturing into unfamiliar territory will naturally motivate you to invest focused effort, conviction, and passion into your work. Passion is a well-known driver of excellence. For example, consider organizing group projects where everyone can contribute ideas. This fosters collaboration and injects fresh perspectives and creativity into your work.

The Power of Asking Questions

Cultivate the habit of asking questions. Not only will you demonstrate active engagement in your work, but you will also impress your superiors with your drive to learn. Asking thoughtful questions broadens your knowledge base and equips you with valuable information. However, the true aim of inquiry should be to unlock your creativity. Be a keen observer, absorb your surroundings, and seek opportunities to express your unique perspective. Expressing your individuality is an art form, and how you choose to invest your efforts reveals a lot about who you are.

40 **PATIENCE IS KEY**

The Power of Patience: Finding Joy Beyond Instant Gratification

David Leonhardt aptly observed, "Instant gratification is not the recipe for happiness." Isn't that true? In today's fast-paced world, fleeting satisfaction can never be as rewarding as the fruits of patience and perseverance.

Do you ever find yourself declaring, "Patience is my biggest enemy?" Living in the 21st century, it is easy to become frustrated with delays and long waiting periods. Ironically, even those "ready-to-eat" meals require some effort (like heating them up) before you can devour them. This simple reality underscores the joy that comes with delayed gratification and enjoying the process.

Some people seem to crave a "new and improved" version of happiness, readily available on demand. However, is happiness truly that fleeting and easily manipulated? Pause and reflect on these questions. The answers might guide you in formulating concrete plans (perhaps for the first time) – at least within your sphere of control. Take time to visualize your desired path in life and ensure it aligns with your true aspirations.

Imagine searching for something important online. You click on a webpage, but it takes five seconds to load. Just five seconds! While you wait, your "instant gratification cells" revolt at the perceived delay. You impulsively jump to another site, only to experience the same frustration. Your impatience leads nowhere, leaving the task unfinished. Had you waited those extra two seconds, you might have achieved your goal.

Life, like your favorite fast food, might not be as enjoyable if you do not allow time for the preparation process. Even a simple pasta dish requires cooking to enhance its flavor. Similarly, your life's significance deepens by dedicating time to personal growth. Avoid hasty decisions that could lead to future regret. Remember, persistence, not haste, is one of life's greatest success formulas.

41 UNFAMILIAR TERRITORY

The Two-Way Street of Happiness: Inner Peace and Spreading Joy

Your conscience is a powerful compass, guiding you towards happiness or unhappiness. Joy is ultimately a choice. Choose to be happy, and it will draw closer to you. Simultaneously, strive to be a source of inspiration and cheerfulness for others, spreading joy like a ripple effect.

Do not wait for external circumstances to dictate your happiness. Step outside your comfort zone and reconnect with your inner self. Release inhibitions and let your authentic personality shine through. Share your happiness with loved ones by throwing a party or simply expressing your genuine spirit. Happiness is not meant to be a solitary pursuit.

Happiness cannot be locked away in isolation. Embrace your talents and share your unique gifts with the world. Continually strive for self-improvement, both at work and home. Go the extra mile and demonstrate your compassion for others. Recognize the significance of inner transformation through mental growth. In essence, break down the walls of isolation and connect with others.

We often encounter people who subscribe to the "live

and let live" philosophy. While cultivating kindness, tolerance, and forgiveness are certainly key components of happiness, the Dalai Lama suggests a two-way street. Helping others can also lead to personal happiness. Acts of service contribute to a more fulfilling existence.

The art of happiness begins with identifying the true sources of joy in your life and setting clear priorities. Balance your inner world with your external reality. Let your internal values and character shine through in your interactions with others. Authenticity and honesty are fundamental to a happy life.

Finally, hold onto your personal values and ethics. These core beliefs should be what truly resonate with you, not mere reflections of external influences. The more clarity you have about your convictions, the greater your happiness and potential for success.

42 SEEKING GROWTH

The Seeds of Happiness: Self-Respect and Chasing Your Dreams

True happiness hinges on a foundation of self-respect and self-appreciation. While excessive indulgence can lead to selfishness, a healthy dose of self-worth is crucial. Within the first few months of introspection, you will likely develop a clearer understanding of your strengths and weaknesses. To command respect and appreciation from others, you must first cultivate a positive self-image.

Ask yourself a critical question: Are you someone you can truly respect and cherish? An affirmative answer indicates significant progress on your path to happiness. However, for many, the answer might be a hesitant "no."

To address this, compare your current self-image with your aspirational self. If there is a gap between these two versions, true happiness remains elusive. While societal norms regarding happiness may hold some value, prioritize self-awareness as your guiding principle. Compare your lifestyle to the general standard of living in your surroundings, but do not yearn for unattainable luxuries. The key is to assess whether you have reached the level you envisioned for yourself.

Consider a situation where you have achieved what society deems "success." Ask yourself: Is this truly what you desired? Have you strayed from your passions and original goals? These are crucial questions on the path to self-improvement. To initiate change, meticulously examine your current lifestyle and identify areas for improvement.

Perhaps there is a long-held dream you have not pursued due to time or resource constraints. To discover your calling, experiment with various activities. Create a flexible schedule that allows you to dedicate time to nurturing existing passions or cultivating new ones.

43 SELF-REFLECTION

Essential Areas for Self-Awareness: Building a Balanced Life

In previous chapters, we discussed essential factors requiring daily management. Some pertain to your home life, while others are strictly personal. It is unwise to force a rigid order on these factors, as unforeseen consequences may arise. As emphasized earlier, the goal of this exercise is to cultivate self-awareness and a positive self-image. With this crucial foundation in place, let us explore some additional key areas in your life.

Personal finances are likely one of the biggest sources of daily worry and concern. We often miscalculate our financial potential, either overestimating or underestimating it. Tracking your finances is crucial. If you are too busy or overwhelmed, seek professional help. Money management is far too practical a matter to leave to chance; left unattended, it can quickly disappear. Mastering debt management is imperative to ensure your debts remain manageable. Creating a smart budget for your personal finances is essential. For example, if you struggle with impulse spending, consider maintaining a steady insurance account. This will provide long-term financial benefits and encourage good saving habits.

Personal health is paramount – it should not become the debilitating factor that hinders your ambitions and dreams. Regular check-ups ensure you stay on top of your physical well-being. Do not ignore bodily symptoms or irregularities, as they might signal an underlying disorder. Engage in regular exercise or sports to enhance mind-body coordination and alleviate the pressures of daily routines. This not only promotes longevity but also fosters a happy, anxiety-free life.

Finally, self-discovery is a continuous journey. Never give up on exploring who you are deep down. The more you embark on self-discovery, the more hidden potential, and talents you will unveil to the world.

44 **MIND MAP**

Embracing Change and Growth: The Power of Journaling

Life's adventures, ups and downs, are often unpredictable. While we cannot foresee everything, we can cultivate a growth mindset and embrace change. After all, as the saying goes, "The show must go on!"

Throughout the day, a multitude of thoughts and plans may flit through your mind. Realistically, you cannot fulfill them all at once. A valuable strategy is to carve out time to record your thoughts about your life path. Journal freely, capturing everything that comes to mind, no matter how trivial (buying groceries, movie tickets, paying bills). Organizing your thoughts on paper grants you space and time to compassionately examine your reactions to them.

Streamlining your life is not about dwelling on past mistakes or self-criticism. Instead, strive to be a mindful observer of your past and present. Similarly, take time to acknowledge the feelings and dreams that arise within you. For example, if you are considering buying a car, jot down the pros and cons. This will aid in making informed decisions.

Reflecting on your personal behaviors, attitudes, and talents that have helped you navigate life is valuable.

Conversely, acknowledging behaviors that may have hindered your pursuit of happiness is equally insightful. This is what it means to live an active and engaged life.

Many famous figures have penned diaries or biographies chronicling both positive and negative experiences. While you may not be a celebrity, the act of journaling can spark immense joy as you discover you have accomplished more than you realized.

If you genuinely seek positive change, an organized approach is an excellent starting point. Instead of being overwhelmed by thoughts, prepare yourself to make well-informed choices and implement effective changes in your life. Journaling fosters awareness of your progress and direction. Think organized, be happy!

45 SHARPEN YOUR INTUITION

Tuning into Your Inner Compass: Intuition for Happiness and Success

How often have you ignored your inner voice, rushing into something only to regret it later? This inner voice, or intuition, is a powerful ally, a guiding force in our lives. Your intuition is an excellent judge of character, events, and situations, nudging you towards the right decisions at the right time. One reason your intuition is so reliable is because it represents your deepest desires and deliberations, free from external influences. So, how can we harness this intuition to achieve true happiness and success? The answer lies in patience, positive thinking, and living a clear, dignified life.

The subconscious mind is a vast reservoir of memories, images, and experiences, a wellspring you can draw from during challenging times. While consciously accessing your subconscious takes practice, you can train it to respond positively to your efforts. To engage your subconscious, leverage the power of positive thinking and sincere intentions. Positive thoughts dispel accumulated negative emotions like stress and anxiety, cleansing your inner self. Your subconscious is the source of ideas, creativity, and deep reflections. To harness its power, you need to make your emotions work for you. For example, if loneliness, sadness, or alienation overwhelm you, channel that energy into passionately pursuing a goal. Hitting the gym with renewed vigor during a difficult period can blast away worries and refocus your life, not to mention giving your biceps a boost!

Intuition is honed by mastering your subconscious mental state. A turbulent mind struggles to register subtle intuitions, shutting you off to opportunities. Imagine yourself in a state of perfect bliss. Using that visualization, feel the world around you come alive. You will likely experience a sense of joy blossoming into heightened awareness of your surroundings. This signifies increased control and interaction with your intuitive faculties. Utilizing this inspired state of mental activity will lead to a clearer understanding of yourself and the world around you.

46 **BE YOUR BEST**

Acting for Self-Improvement: Practical Steps for a Better You

In previous chapters, we discussed factors to consider on your self-improvement journey. However, these factors come into play only when you delve into the "how" and "why" of your life. For most, a practical approach to self-improvement yields the best results. This refers to steps that can be seamlessly integrated into your daily schedule.

Building a better you start with transforming your current self. Identify tasks that enhance your focus on this goal. If you are not physically fit, explore the benefits of exercise. Find a gym near you and create a schedule that complements your routine. Remember, building muscle is not the sole purpose – aim for a well-rounded workout that tones your body while promoting muscle development. Exercise can also improve health for those who are obese or have conditions like high blood pressure or a weakened immune system. And let us not forget the motivational power of seeing a toned physique every morning!

Your enthusiasm – your passions and hobbies – define who you are. To get more out of life, examine these passions critically. Consider how you can contribute to society. For instance, if you are passionate about fiction, you could open a local lending library for children or encourage book clubs among young people in your area. If you love soccer, you could help launch a free soccer clinic in your community. The key is to love what you do and share that passion with others.

Developing interests becomes easier once you understand your preferences. There is a world of exciting and intriguing things waiting to be explored. Invest time and effort in your positive obsessions, and you will reap rich rewards.

47 **FOLLOW YOUR HEART**

Finding Your Passion: The Key to Happiness

There is more to the desire for a happy life than immediate wants. Ultimately, everyone strives for happiness, which unites us.

The key to happiness lies within – in discovering your passion. The answer does not lie in external validation. Do not compare your life to others' standards; happiness is the only true measure. Passions have no hierarchy or monetary value. It might be the small art pieces you create at home or the business empire you built. The crucial element is the deep exploration required to uncover your passion. Let your inner voice be your guide.

The path to success in your area of passion may have twists and turns. However, two things remain constant: hard work and self-belief. Do not crumble in the face of difficulties. The obstacles you encounter are tests of character and resilience. If you are passionate about what you do, you will find a way to overcome them. Develop a "bulldog mentality," as the British would say – unwavering determination.

However, perseverance needs to be balanced with pragmatism. A well-defined plan is essential for excelling in your field. Do not rush into commitments without planning, and strive for non-confrontational solutions. Maintain a goal-oriented approach to evaluate your performance and fuel your drive.

And celebrate your achievements! Reward yourself for hitting your targets.

The key to joy in life does not lie in imitation. We are all unique individuals with distinct talents. Everyone has something they excel at. Remember, you are not beholden to anyone else's judgment. If something resonates with you emotionally and is worth your investment, pursue it.

Happiness is your birthright, and this is the path to achieving it.

48 CRAFT YOUR CORE BELIEFS

Finding Your Passion: The Key to Happiness

There is more to the desire for a happy life than immediate wants. Ultimately, everyone strives for happiness, which unites us all.

The key to happiness lies within you – in discovering your passion. The answer does not reside in external validation. Do not compare your life to others' standards; happiness is the only true measure. Passions have no hierarchy or monetary value. It might be the little art pieces you create at home or the business empire you built on your own. The crucial element is the deep exploration required to uncover your passion. Let your inner voice be your guide.

The path to success in your area of passion may have twists and turns. However, two things remain constant: hard work and self-belief. Do not crumble in the face of difficulties. The obstacles you encounter are tests of character and resilience. If you are passionate about what you do, you will find a way to overcome them. Develop a "bulldog mentality," as the British would say – unwavering determination.

However, perseverance needs to be balanced with pragmatism. A well-defined plan is essential for excelling in your field. Do not rush into commitments without planning, and strive for solutions that avoid creating conflict. Maintain a goal-oriented approach to evaluate your performance and fuel your drive.

And celebrate your achievements! Reward yourself for hitting your targets.

The key to joy in life does not lie in imitation. We are all unique individuals with distinct talents. Everyone excels at something. Remember, you are not beholden to anyone else's judgment. If something resonates with you emotionally and is worth your investment, pursue it.

Happiness is your birthright, and this is the path to achieving it.

49 INNER JOY: A SELF-DISCOVERY PATH

Joy, that elusive emotion, often seems tethered to external circumstances – a dream job, a perfect relationship, a luxurious vacation. Yet, true, and lasting happiness often blossoms from a more fertile ground: the wellspring within ourselves. Finding joy within is a journey of self-discovery, a practice of cultivating gratitude, and a commitment to nurturing our passions.

The first step on this inward exploration is self-awareness. We must identify what truly brings us a sense of fulfillment. This might involve revisiting long-forgotten hobbies, experimenting with new activities, or simply paying closer attention to the moments that spark a flicker of delight within us. Does getting lost in a good book transport you? Does the rhythm of creating art soothe your soul? Does spending time in nature leave you feeling refreshed? By identifying these wellsprings of intrinsic joy, we can begin to weave them into the fabric of our daily lives.

Gratitude is another potent tool for cultivating inner joy. So often, we become accustomed to the good things in our lives, failing to truly appreciate them. Taking a moment each day to reflect on what we are grateful for, whether it is a steaming cup of coffee, a supportive friend, or simply the ability to breathe deeply, shifts our perspective and allows us to savor the present moment. This practice of mindful appreciation fosters a sense of contentment that transcends external circumstances.

Finally, nurturing our passions is essential for finding joy within. When we engage in activities that ignite our curiosity or tap into our creative potential, we enter a state of flow, a state of complete absorption and enjoyment. This does not require grand gestures; it can be as simple as dedicating time to writing, playing music, learning a new skill, or simply spending time in nature. By carving out space for these pursuits, we nourish a part of ourselves that brings immense joy and a sense of purpose.

Finding joy within is not about ignoring life's challenges. It is about cultivating a sense of inner resilience that allows us to weather storms and find pockets of happiness even amidst difficulties. It is about recognizing that true joy is not a destination, but a journey – a journey of self-discovery, gratitude, and passionate engagement with the world around us. It is a journey that starts within, and its rewards are immeasurable.

50 **GROW WITH THE FLOW**

Embracing Change and Growth: A Guide to Personal Well-being

As new discoveries are made and uncharted territories explored in personal care and well-being, innovative and exciting lifestyles are emerging, replacing older ones. Subtle shifts are happening all around you, directly or indirectly impacting your life. Within this constant flux, it is entirely up to you to discover your own joy and contribute positively to this evolving landscape.

All forms of change and habit modification must originate from within. Mastering your own abilities, intellect, and resources is essential for navigating this transformation. By taking on the challenge of self-improvement, you automatically set in motion a positive ripple effect in the world around you. In the journey of self-empowerment, it is never too late to begin.

Start by identifying known shortcomings that might hinder you from reaching your full potential. Strive to build a habitual resistance to addictions such as alcoholism, nicotine dependence, tobacco use, and the like. This effort will not only empower you to live a healthier life but also equip you to make firm personal decisions.

If you have been neglecting any physical issues, no matter how minor they may seem, now is the time to seek professional medical advice. A seemingly insignificant spasm, sprain, or chest pain is best addressed promptly. Delaying treatment will only jeopardize your well-being and potentially that of your family.

Organization is another crucial element deserving your focused attention. It is a vital factor in managing the various aspects that contribute to your growth and success. Smart resource allocation and effective time management not only conserve your efforts and resources but also ensure optimal returns on your investments. Integrating these practices into your life might seem daunting initially, but with improved organization, they will become second nature.

Therefore, prioritize effectively and dedicate your time and effort accordingly. Once you care enough about your daily life, you will begin to anticipate what it has in store for you.

AFTERWORD

Finally, if you found this information valuable, please consider leaving an honest review of this book on Amazon. Your thoughts and opinions are highly appreciated.

Wishing you all the best,

Alex Bedoya

ABOUT THE AUTHOR

Alex Giovanni Bedoya's journey is a testament to resilience and kindness. Born in Colombia, he endured poverty and homelessness in the bustling streets of New York City since age 16. Despite the challenges, he remained untainted by trouble, drugs, or smoke. With a heart of gold and an outgoing spirit, he embraced the world with open arms, extending help to anyone in need. His selfless acts of compassion, fueled by his love for humanity and nature, inspired friends to urge him into writing. Now, his words echo globally, a beacon of hope and empathy.